# THOUGHTS THAT

## Set Me Free

# THOUGHTS THAT

## Set Me Free

An anthology of poetry and quotes that liberated my soul

## SAACHI RAJIV DEVNANI

First published in India in 2016 by Kiwi Books

Copyright © 2016 Saachi Rajiv Devnani

ISBN 978–93–86301–10–9

BISG Code: POE000000 POETRY / General

Typesetting and cover design: Kiwi Books

Kiwi Books
an imprint of Dogears Print Media Pvt. Ltd.
Plot No 16, Housing Board Colony
Gogol, Margao
Goa 403601 India
www.cinnamonteal.in

*To those who made my journey tough,*
*Some more enjoying my moments rough,*
*How do I forget who were by my side,*
*Best of them is my Mr. Right.*

*Special thanks to my cousin, Heena Dilip Bhatia, who seeded the thought of digitizing and publishing what was only a part of my personal diary.*

# QUOTES FILLED IN LITTLE NOTES

When you decide to be happy everything you've lost comes back chasing you.

For our reality to meet our desires, we must unlearn the pain of our current existence and absorb the delight of our dreams.

The best opportunities never appear in our direct vision, for they come to those who dare to see differently than the rest.

That which is of the most value will not be found until you dive into what others won't even step over.

Saachi Rajiv Devnani

Our true test is to spot happiness when it is least visible.

Innocence can only be fooled. Its purity can never be touched by the filth of evil.

I'm so grateful for the moments that caused turbulence in my life because they catapulted me to the best times ever.

You know the best days of your life are imminent just when you're going through the worst.

Don't let your wishes be like bubbles that lose existence under external force. Give them the strength of stones so they destroy everything that tries to break them.

You don't have to be educated to be talented.

Happiness is often misunderstood. We want to find it in things, people, and events while it waits within us, hoping to be recognized.

Saachi Rajiv Devnani

We only fail to be happy because we do not allow joy to touch us as easily as we permit ourselves to be hurt.

The most beautiful moments of our life arrive when we open the doors of our mind with utmost faith.

The authenticity of our thoughts is measured by our intentions for the outcome of those thoughts.

If it wasn't for those trying to pull me back, I would have never made an effort to move forward.

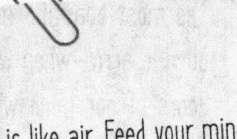

Happiness is like air. Feed your mind with it - the weight is never felt yet its presence makes all the difference.

Those who work don't "show". Those who "show", don't work.

We are living in a time when fake people are as common as fake goods.

A corrupt soul's bad intentions cannot be hidden with a fake layer of innocence.

Sometimes, we turn people into what we want them to be and call it love.

We become fearless when we know we have nothing to lose.

A lie always needs a soft voice. the truth is never scared to be loud.

What someone does once is appreciated forever but what you've been doing forever is not appreciated even once.

At times, the image we create to show the world is a lie we are telling ourselves.

Seeing through those who are pretending is as easy as looking through glass because both don't have any substance.

The sweetest tongue causes the widest barriers and deepest cuts.

Get yourself addicted to being happy and no obstacle will be able to stop you from fulfilling your dreams.

It is easy to be good for a day or two.
Being good forever is a virtue of few.

Every day in our life comes once in a lifetime.

Losing integrity to safeguard your image indicates a weak character.

The absence of some people brings the presence of happiness in life.

Diverting the mind from what disturbs you most is the key to unlocking the door to happiness.

As the number of fakes increase, the real ones get doubted too.

Those who compete with others never win. The competition is always with ourselves.

Some devils are born in the form of humans; they create hell wherever they go.

The best way to accept some of the worst behaved people is to know that one day karma will get hold of them.

Don't prove them wrong, just prove yourself to be right and the world will see.

Revenge is bitter, karma is sweet. Choose your taste wisely.

People who buy you things are spending what they will earn back. Those who give you their time are spending what will never return.

Sometimes you come to a point where being fake becomes so natural that you forget what it was like to be real.

When the feelings and intentions behind a wish are genuine, it gets granted.

The best days of your life always come right after the worst.

When you've tolerated being suppressed, they'll never accept your rising.

If you obey you'll always be a victim, if you rebel you'll always rule.

Irony of life:
> Work like a donkey and get treated like one.
> Relax like a king, and you'll be given a royal service.
> Conclusion: the way we treat ourselves is the way people treat us.

How you conduct yourself as an adult is a reflection of what you were taught as a child.

There's so much you can do to beautify a face, yet nothing to cover an ugly heart.

What you're most arrogant about will be taken away,
What you're most thankful for will remain forever.

When you've dreamt of something but not asked for it from anyone, yet it falls in your hands like an unexpected rain shower, you know you've been doing the right thing.

Saachi Rajiv Devnani

Those who take revenge everyday for what happened in the past, have imprisoned themselves for a lifetime.

The people you shelter the most will be the ones to leave you first.

Our life is a direct reflection of what we hold inside us. Being miserable and bitter only recreates similar experiences in life.

It's good when you've been slapped, kicked, pushed, and trampled repeatedly because thereafter nothing ever hurts anymore and that's how happiness is achieved.

Love is not about how many times you nod in agreement to please your partner. It is about how well you balance your disagreements without the fear of disappointing them.

Much like gadgets, I wish we could set a reminder in our minds each time we are good to someone who has hurt us over and over again.

It is not love if it transforms you into what the other person wants you to be.

A villain's interference is necessary to prove yourself a hero.

Our bodies are similar to machinery – if not put to continuous use, they rot to become inoperable.

A bruised history is an invalid justification for current misbehavior.

Carriers of inner peace can survive the harshest terrains..

Stubbornness is like an adhesive. The longer it stays on you, the tougher it is to remove.

Accusing everyone but yourself for a shattered state of mind is like dismissing our own responsibilities and criminalizing the innocent.

Our mind and a USB drive are alike. Storing old unusable data allows no space for updated, relevant information.

If change were a bad attribute we would continue to remain in The Stone Age.

# POETRY

Like the early morning chant,
Your presence fills peace,
Purifying my moments,
That once felt heavy.
You're the soul of truth,
A rare finding on earth,
Among treasures and jewels,
Beyond you nothing is worth.

As my memories wander
Through the streets of love,
They thank their stars
And heavens above.
For bringing you to Earth
Just for me,
Like an unfinished puzzle's
Missing piece.

The only one to move the needle
Of my empty joy tank,
Beyond the limits of FULL.
It's too much for me to thank
Good deeds of previous birth,
Prayers on sleepless nights,
Wonder what worked for me,
To find my Mr. Right.

∽

Our paths may not meet,
The tracks separate our feet,
Yet when I lose balance,
I expect your hand in silence.
Go away yet be close,
Like a comfort zone in my lows.
Parallel journeys don't mean distance,
Just keep me tied with your love's existence.

Saachi Rajiv Devnani

My definition of love
Starts and ends with you,
Nothing beneath and above
Will ever be so true.

Without the need to search,
My love story was written.
Giving a space to perch,
With romance it was litten.

Painting my life with beauty,
Creating a masterpiece,
You're my priceless reward,
I'd hold on to for eternity.

While walking alone
In the lane of love,
A stranger came my way.
I wondered about his intentions,
Why he brought smiles to my day.

Drowned in confusion and doubt
I went with him ahead,
And seeing his rare innocence,
Understood the feelings unsaid.

As we moved miles further,
A realization I could feel.
And I knew that very moment,
He was the one made for me.

The end had come to a gloomy phase
That for years had eclipsed my life.
And he made the world around me
As beautiful as paradise.

Saachi Rajiv Devnani

With you my smile
Goes an extra mile.
Your tough surface
Doesn't leave a trace,
Of the romance you hold,
Hidden beneath the folds.

The charm so mighty,
Melts me completely.
No less than a legend,
Our love will leave a trend.

Some years ago it took birth
In the corner of my heart.
Wondered if it should be grown
Or forgotten and torn apart.

Then came a voice from the heavens
It sounded like God to me.
He said it's love I've gifted you with;
Let this emotion within be.

So special I thought I was
To be his Chosen one.
To protect this precious feeling
In a way very few had done.

As it grew like a child so sweet,
I reared it with all my care.
And felt the touch of purity,
Of this sentiment so rare.

Some wounds from the past are so deep
That they haven't healed in years.
People notice yet haven't changed,
Even today they bring me tears.

When the heart has never seen love
It's only gone through pain,
Emotions die an unknown death
And numbness fills in every vein.

As I watch the world around
Everyone's moving ahead,
While my lonely soul's at standstill
And my lucky stars are dead.

Echoes of painful cries
Trapped in the walls of my heart,
Begging for mercy and release
Time doesn't let them depart.

I'm waiting along with them,
For a miracle to fulfill my dreams.
Hoping the emptiness fades,
So forever we can live in peace.

In my dreamland a house I've built,
Where I often go to hide.
Fancying we'll live together,
Allowing love to join and reside.

The glass roof will give way
To the twinkling starlit sky,
While we take a chance to embrace
And be amazed as we lie.

Soothing breeze knocking on the windows,
Waiting to be welcomed by us.
It'll touch the walls and fill our hearts
With tons of happiness.

Saachi Rajiv Devnani

Like a pair of love
Designed to be one,
With merged perspectives,
And a common direction.

The vision is clear,
Nothing to fear,
Beautiful is this journey,
Just Romance, You, and Me.

Feeling his little fingers rested on my face,
The warmth of his pure, most innocent embrace.
Wish time would halt till this joy lasts,
Let today not become a day in my past.

The smaller his appearance, the deeper his love,
Unmatched to the paradise and heavens above.
An award I've received for my noble deeds,
His mommy is all I want to be.

Saachi Rajiv Devnani

Dark shadows of loneliness
Pierce through her smiles,
Yearning his constant presence,
The distance seems in miles.

She dreamt that the joy
Would forever stay,
To spend their time together,
But the spark has faded away.

Has time played black magic,
Or has she gone wrong?
To lose him bit by bit,
While her worth keeps going down.

∽

Constant supply of people who hurt,
An ever-flowing stream of painful remarks.
Unstoppable rush of lies over truth,
That promise to keep me in the dark.

Saachi Rajiv Devnani

And then one day,
They'll have no say,
As karma walks in
To wipe their sins.

What you carelessly do today
Will never go away.
And if there's no tomorrow,
Your next life will borrow.

Like a burden so heavy,
You'll be forced to carry.
Then will come regret,
Because karma never forgets.

The rule of life is such,
Good people get cut first.
And those who are of evil made,
Get to enjoy the comfort of shade.

Innocence loses the battle each time,
Reward is taken away by crime,
Purity is never believed,
From pain it won't be ever relieved.

Tales of a broken soul,
Buried by forced smiles,
Longing the touch of pure joy,
It chooses to take a while.

Hidden behind sounds of laughter,
Is a dying ray of Hope.
Battling against the power of lies,
It's lost the chance to cope.

Don't let the light within
Blow out with the storms.
Those who create them
Know only how to harm.

Shine like a lamp
No matter how little you are.
They see themselves as superior,
Yet they're too dark to come at par.

Saachi Rajiv Devnani

Every time I get chopped for telling the truth,
I rearrange myself and get knocked down again,
Only to realize the world is impressed by the glamour of lies,
While truth will get concealed in its simplicity.

A lie is a short-lived thrill,
Truth needs a stronger will.
The first round dishonesty wins,
Yet the sincere takes over who sins.

Saachi Rajiv Devnani

The day has arrived,
When truth beats lie.
Goodness rises above evil,
Innocence sees the victory,
Purity takes the rule.
May this happen everyday,
To lighten up our shaded way.

Jealousy incubates revenge,
Revenge showcases inferiority.
Those busy harming others,
Only talk the language of enmity.

The hostility spreads,
While peace craves to multiply.
Unless the ugly heart changes,
Togetherness will continue to die.

Can I fly,
Like this balloon so high?
Escaping those
I never chose
To surround me.
They only empty
My joyful heart.
Let me depart,
Release the weight,
Before it's too late.

❧

Living with devils
Don't bring down your level.
They're born with a mind,
The focus is to grind,
Your peace and pride.
Their souls have died,
Don't hope for them to awaken,
The purpose was to shaken,
All that you've built.
Not feeling any guilt,
Be strong enough,
So they forget to laugh,
At the fallen pieces.
As time releases,
The courage you hold,
Let it secretly unfold.

Saachi Rajiv Devnani

By being untrue,
You may get through,
And win the race,
With a shameless face.
Some day a mirror,
Will reflect the fear,
When the past comes chasing,
While you're heedlessly grazing,
Oblivious of your deeds,
Selfishly stuffing your needs,
The horror won't get over,
You'll not have space for cover.

Wrapped in the storms of blame,
My sincerity put to flames,
A two-faced crew came marching,
The soul was flustered, arching,
Torture coming from a distance,
Faithful reasoning none to listen,
The air absorbs all agony,
They've sworn to turn me lonely,
Victory decides to join them,
While I'm imprisoned in the hall of shame.

Saachi Rajiv Devnani

Playing hide and seek,
Emotions gone bleak,
They've gone underground,
Secrets not to be found.
A layer I've assembled,
Access not enabled,
The depth beyond my walls,
Present endless falls.
Do not touch the mysteries,
It's all a part of history.

Worshipping your brilliance,
Crumbled my despair.
A daunting survival,
What I dreaded, now impaired.
Winds that you stroke,
Transform disturbed climates.
Clearing frosted hurdles,
Breathtaking journey emanates.
Driving within boundaries,
Of your aura marvellous,
Enclose me eternally,
Turning my fate to auspicious.

Saachi Rajiv Devnani

Reciting heroic fables,
My purpose carrying their label,
Galloping in a direction blind,
A mountain I picked to climb.
Stubbornly visioning pinnacle,
Like a warrior invincible,
Day or night irrelevant,
Treasure of blessings prevalent,
Fueled my pace with zeal,
Reaching fantasies felt surreal.

ﾟ

Dipped in pools of trance,
Offering whims that warrant a dance,
Untouched their galaxy,
Blossoming vitality,
Swaying sensations shine,
Emitting waves divine,
Super-charged each atom,
Madness impossible to fathom.

Soiled by the outcome
Of their arrogant acts,
The stench of vengeance
Has coated all facts.
My morals and truth
Are falsely handcuffed,
Behind an illusion of sweetness,
They're powerfully submerged.

Yet the core of my mind,
Plays a melody of hope,
Obscuring scenes of nightmares,
Faith has some scope.
Illuminating my perseverance,
The malicious left an effect,
Accelerating countless desires,
My capacity it failed to detect.

Lost in the chambers of gloom,
Uninvited I landed at doom,
Gates to glittering glee,
Locked without a key.
The scheme was deliberate,
Devils craving to celebrate,
A fabricated triumph,
They perceive themselves as giants.
Bloated by hollow pride,
Splashing droplets of snide,
An attempt to slaughter my aim,
The craze they wish to tame,
Ignorant of intense passion,
Those faint-hearted can't crash in,
With fences high and wide,
I have karma by my side.

Saachi Rajiv Devnani

Sailing through deep waters,
Ignorant of breezing destiny,
Emerged an army of deceit,
Un-cautioned by reality.
They crept up in silence,
Camouflaged by restless waves,
Undermining my vigor,
Assured I'll not be saved.
Ill-equipped for the barriers,
Supplied with integrity,
Their might was deficient,
My base was sturdy.
Startled by the defeat,
For a conflict unplanned,
At the dawn of realization,
We saw the horizon expand.

৩

Scorching rays of disdain,
Uncovered, obstructed lanes,
A maze with revenge constructed,
Slyly, exits deducted.
What made them think I'll stay,
Won't let my resilience decay.
Brimming with assurance,
Reviving batches of tolerance,
Gateway to freedom is near.
Visualizing a finale clear,
Magnetic energy steering me,
It propelled my faith to eternity.

Saachi Rajiv Devnani

Lies each day,
Within I fray,
How were they made?
Dignity for trade,
To adopt glamour,
A tainted flavour,
Of stagnant conscience,
Their unique license,
Of transmitting grief,
Like a ruthless chief.
Impotent sentiments,
Their angels dormant,
Underrating dynamics,
Their souls metallic,
Unable to touch,
The fantasy to clutch,
My immovable strength.
Conveying their end,
A persistent flame,
Erased their name.

Draped in the cradle of peace,
Ecstasy refusing to cease,
Splendor of being unmarred,
Entrance for enmity barred,
Air swirling with bliss,
Serenity giving a kiss,
Portions of goodness rooted,
Leisurely they've fruited,
Floating in placid emotions,
Smoothly passing commotion,
Signs of strain dissolved,
Worries of future resolved.

Bestowed luxuries of freedom,
Occasional occurring season,
Arousing a latent appetite,
My frozen willpower stood upright.
Aspirations eagerly woken,
Widening wings once broken,
Soaring lightly in glory,
Forming a trail, my story,
The envious wore a frown,
Spectating me being crowned.

Lingering at the doorstep,
For elation to disembark,
A surprise presented,
I suspected a lark.
Extending their base,
Ready to accelerate,
Grabbing my feet,
The clouds exhilarate.
Mounting naturally,
Gravity can't halt,
Against all forces,
We landed by a vault.
Empty was its space,
Private message written,
"Don't search around,
Just glance within".

Saachi Rajiv Devnani

Swings of time fluctuate,
Inner peace I circulate,
Unclogging routes from lumps,
Slumbered arteries pumped,
Radiance has surfaced,
With tranquility laced,
Treatment not required,
The source now rewired,
Restoring knotted tracks,
Like a magnet, pleasure I attract.

That muscled frame,
Tireless he trains,
A zest endless,
With power excess.
Yet a child resides,
In a corner inside,
Longing to play,
Freedom all day,
Striking a balance,
Immense the challenge,
Regardless he picked,
What others left un-ticked.

Laughter she shows,
As her grief grows,
Anxious to solve,
May all thorns dissolve.
Tears don't store,
There's an outlet to pour,
Vacate the space,
Don't leave a trace.
Let happiness accrue,
Feel the real you.

Causing floods of accuses,
Defending void excuses,
Words made of grime,
Consciously inflicting crime.
Insolence studded soul,
Eclipsed horrid goal,
Who sculptured them as human,
Ethics and values loosened,
Re-fixing is effort in vain,
Their ambition is selfish gain.

ॐ

The Goddess of wealth,
Abundantly graced them,
Holding intentions of greed,
Their activities did stem,
Unaware of a vicious circle,
It filters motives of damage,
Tossing back what they discarded,
Creating rebound for ravage.
Blinded by exaggeration,
Of deceptive self-righteousness,
They staggered confidently,
Preserving a character spineless.

Their body wants to rest,
Physical work is a guest.
Momentum swiftly eroded,
Lethargy fully loaded,
Emerged symptoms of rust,
Heaps gathered of dust.
They've lost the ability to shed,
Diseased willingness now dead,
Like an engine defective,
Prolonged era inactive,
Bundles of comfort amassed,
Life's trials they failed to pass.

Empty handed at birth,
Greeted by the universe,
Tenderly caressing,
Selflessly it nurtures.
Ungrateful humankind,
Alters the priority list,
Materialistic pleasures,
Driving forces of his quest.
Maturing with age,
The cracks deepen,
Breaking a default bond,
Disconnection creeps in.
Approaching the closure,
He ponders over bygones,
Those possessions he relished,
He was farewelled all alone.

Shrinking her morals,
To elevate an image,
Envisioning the aftermath,
She initiated carnage.
Blackened all her virtues,
Shrewdness advised,
Eradicate the honoured,
Drop your elegance to rise.
Her rule shortly conquered,
Backfired tricks for a throne,
Losing the estimate,
Deception cost her a fortune.

Saachi Rajiv Devnani